ANATOMY, ERRATA

Winner of the 1997 Ohio State University Press/
The Journal Award in Poetry

ANATOMY, ERRATA

POEMS BY
JUDITH HALL

Ohio State University Press
Columbus

Library of Congress Cataloging-in-Publication Data
Hall, Judith, 1951–
    Anatomy, errata / Judith Hall.
        p.   cm.
    "Winner of the 1997 Ohio State University Press/The journal award in poetry."
    ISBN 0-8142-0764-2 (cloth : alk. paper). —ISBN 0-8142-0765-0
(paper : alk. paper)
        1. Breast—Cancer—Patients—Poetry 2. Mothers and daughters—
Poetry. 3. Women patients—Poetry. 4. Women—Poetry.   I. Title.
    PS3558.A3695A83   1998
    811'.54—dc21   98-21372
                                                              CIP

Text design: Donna Hartwick.
Jacket design: Alec Bernstein and Monika Zych.
Jacket illustration: Courtesy Museum of Fine Arts, Boston.
Type set in Adobe Garamond.
Printed by McNaughton & Gunn.

The paper used in this publication meets the minimum requirements of the American
National Standard for Information Sciences—Permanence of Paper for Printed Library
Materials.
ANSI Z39.48-1992.

9 8 7 6 5 4 3 2 1

Acknowledgments

Grateful acknowledgment is made to the editors of the following publications, in which these poems first appeared, often in somewhat different forms:

Colorado Review: "Bergman's Cancer," "Temple"
The Journal: "Reflections Lost in the Ladies' Room," "Touched Relics," "Godmother's Will"
The New Republic: "Interior with Metal Instruments"
The Paris Review: "Was It" (under the title "A Lullaby"), "Ink and Green Wash: In the Oncologist's Waiting Room" (under the title "Reruns in the Oncologist's Waiting Room"), "Rimbaud's Cancer," "Stamina"
Ploughshares: "The Other Girls in Lettuce"
Southwest Review: "To Come with Accessories"
Western Humanities Review: "The Monarch Birthmark," "St. Peregrinus' Cancer"

"St. Peregrinus' Cancer" also appeared in *The Best American Poetry 1995*, edited by Richard Howard and David Lehman (Simon & Schuster, 1995).

"Descendent" appeared in the anthology *What Will Suffice: Contemporary American Poets on the Art of Poetry*, edited by Christopher Buckley and Christopher Merrill (Gibbs Smith, 1995).

For Alec Bernstein

Contents

                                        Yet, trudging
                      on two legs that move contradictorily,
          irked by ghosts and witches, one
                                does not fear to ask for beauty

that is power devoid of fear.

                                —MARIANNE MOORE

The Monarch Birthmark

Eyelash kisses: "Moth goodnight." Her lashes tickle:
    Monarchs kiss me
Off to sleep. And "Meadow Copper," "Sleepy Orange"
    Butterfly goodnight. The fluttered kisses quiver

        Cheek and chin. And silver checker-
        Spots on nose; the calicoes; a "Luna"
    Laughing; kiss me
        Here and here. Goodnight, the swarming

        Viceroys and
    Silverspots; the lips of clicking
Wings. Again she says goodnight. And
    Are there moths of caraway

And moths of Switzerland and swallowtails,
    "Alfalfa," "Western Sister"?
        Feed on baby's breath
                and cherry,
Sycamore and ash, and drink the puddled mud and

    Milkweed, honey
Sage. The green-dust kisses brush; ask her anything
    To stay. She moves across me; slower, blue-black robe,
    Voluminous with butterflies,

        Gauloise-perfumed; the pearly eyes,
    Their eye-spots, knots,
        Drop; open downy orange ears,
        And tickle here.

Hug; another minute; other
Lullabies of butterflies; kiss
    The zebras, banded purples,
Pygmies. "Are you sleeping?" Blink below her

    Reading voice, a whisper-watch;
        Slower, lower stirs
            a vowel
Breaks, waving clouds good-bye and branches, blankets, leaves,
   "I said it's time."

Another minute—"Monarch" clouds of kisses; quick;
    Lift among the giddy, amber rabble, rising
        Up to covering evergreens. Caress
      The trees in Mexico they choose

    For sleep. And sleep,
        Their wings up; lacy underthings—
      "But why?" She stays
Another minute; "Monarch" kisses.

Lashes tickle. Now a chilly
    Juice: A sleepy orange with
Her cigarette and remnants of Chanel.
    She hovers by the bed, not

        Sitting, standing now,
              enormous
Robe of "Admiral," "Diana"; shivers pour her
    Sleeves across her
Chest, dark as every hall behind her. She would dart

Away at any minute; any, anything
        To stop her, like a funny song:
        "Tick tock / Tickle talk / Tickle you!"
"Now that's enough."

        Down comes baby, the hand falling
        Hard on her face,
    Hit. She had to hit me, had to,
She explained, as lips, a scarlet

    Wave, recede. The dolls, awake
On pillows, stiffen, watching the whole sky.
        Our nature secret. We are
                Strange enough to keep,

                        prepared in

A "relaxing jar": My specimens of silence
        Pinned. Skin accepts
And then adopts the pin. The pleasure waking hurt,
        A secret song.

The Other Girls in Lettuce

These are the reminiscent lettuces,
And girls with pockets full of teeth
Will disappear in them, in fields of watered lettuce.
They sing when no one watches them in lettuce.
"Love what no one else would love. No one
Else would do it." They dot the far rows of lettuce,
Scavengers, enamored of the lettuces:
Their rapid filling out in light; and loud
When broken, loved and broken. The loudest
Mastication! Jaws ache in opened lettuce,
As they pick the blushing heads and hide.
If girls are eating, they will have to hide.

They mob the hazel shadows and they hide,
Stuffing their mouths with early lettuces,
With pampered butterheads; radicchios; they hide
With escarole, bending smaller; hide.
They had to do it—grab her with their teeth
And tear the subcutaneous fat. O make them hide!
What was chosen, what was trash, and what will hide?
Distant mother, distant girls. No one
Wants to hear what they did. No one
Hears them lick pretty lips in hiding.
Because the pinkest girls are not allowed
To hunger, touching thighs to come. Not allowed.

No blood on thighs or thoughts allowed
Except in hiding. "Alleluia!" In hiding,
This aberrance—this ravaging allowed.
She tasted like an afterlife allowed.
Then palate cleansers: Vinegar on lettuces,
Vinegar on massive greens allowed.
Did they do it? Was her death allowed?
No one knew the girls who did it with their teeth,
Who held her down; cut, tearing open; teeth
Devoured her. Alleged longing can be loud
And trembling; a pain known,
In dreams, as what they wanted to forget; no—

They wanted that preemptive banquet, but no
Tattletales of loneliness allowed.
They murmur, breathy moppet voices: "No one
Else would chew until it bleeds"; and know
They did it; fear it; diet; carry the fear in hiding:
Fury squeezed to a squeaking no one knows.
Call it giggling, and no one knows.
The future can be eaten like the past, with lettuce
And a cartoon vinaigrette, a tiny tune for lettuce.
No one questioned waking girls. No one
Claimed her body. No identifying teeth.
Shhh: Their pockets kept her gathered teeth

A secret. There, they pet her teeth,
Holding them as baby cups for tears. They know
Their curves, charms, and lick her teeth,
Tasting such possession. She left them all her teeth.
And days of anorexic industry, singing, loud,
"Grinding love to lettuce with our teeth!"
A half-remembered whistle couples air and teeth.
Never there; they play at blaming her and hide.
And love to think of her, hiding
In their love. They kiss the bracelets of her teeth:
The ivory on ivory, a luscious
Subterfuge; imagined matricide and lettuces.

Daughters want to stay with their lettuces
And work, the awful work they do in hiding,
Hushing appetites. They whisper, clenching teeth,
"Love her more than anyone." Anyone knows
Words are nipples still allowed.

At Play with Purity

A girl's lips rehearse with silent, silent puckers.
Invented kisses visit; visits unreturned.
Her doll excels at nonexistent conversations.
A girl's lips rehearse with silent, silent puckers
For her heroine, her doll—what Simone de Beauvoir
Called her "natural plaything, penis . . . bandaged finger."
A girl's lips rehearse, with silent, silent puckers,
Invented kisses. Visit. Visits unreturned.

Godmother's Will

At the family reunion, the academic
Was discussed, his future
And engagement to one of the best daughters.
Aunts dissected him,
Ambling on, dropping their swizzle sticks
Into their sister's artificial pond.
They spied his borrowed, superfluous Armani tie. He flinched,
Forgetting his remark.

The hostess pulled lupine from her peachblow tureen.
He stood too close to her.
She tapped his shirt and said, "Never presume,"
And smiled so he would leave, heartened or
Humiliated, whichever he preferred.
And when he did leave, then, she confided,
To the family's prolonged, habitual applause,
Her precarious escape.

They remember her dismissive gossip, the reflected glory
Of acquaintances in Europe.
"As Marlene always said to me—"
The child clapped again
And hung by her godmother's Versace,
Mouthing along, "I remember Stockholm,
When Greta's scoliosis was a rumor. Those jokes
Among the prop boys!

Never slouch and never hire witty sons of friends."
"Or me," the daughter laughed,
But it petered out, a burp alone.
"Ungrateful," her godmother smiled
And turned to fresher ears. "Did you mention—?
I knew the poor dear in Paris, before
She *finally* bleached her forearm hair"; and voices flickered in
Resulting lethargy.

"The consensus was she was too tall; a mouth, too full and vulvate.
'Mystery, Jacqueline'—
I told her to avoid interviews—
'Mystery succeeds,
In a regressive age, the art of conversation.'"
Her words seemed suspended, like the perfect
Little orchids, adapted to the peachblow tureen.
The child listened forever.

Everything else she thought she knew appeared and disappeared
Except her, her godmother,
Her coruscating scorn, her reassuring
Superiority.
And laughter orbited derision; laughter
Was her glory. Any change from this,
The child knew, was betrayal, and she would have to leave,
As he did, and he was sad.

Touched Relics

A mother's amber necklaces and pearls—
In the season almost past,
When supplicants
Arranged their token slipper shells,
Rejoicing in the feasts of fruit liqueurs
With pomegranates,
Seven fennel seeds—
Were memorized, like legends of her dignity.
And those who worshipped her with chanterelles
And orange water,
Artichokes they steamed in clay,
Knew that miracles confirmed were such a comfort.
Our lady of the cocktail hats and silk pajamas.
*

The bleeding willow

Observed by widowers
So grateful for a sign; for tulips reminiscent
Of her preferences
Or of her sorrow.
*

The mystical tradition recommends,
"If you cannot have her breast, have her sorrow."
Or have a cloth she held;
A relic. Handkerchiefs were sold
Beyond the saint's neglected tomb.
You know the one—whose beauty made her suffering
Exemplary, who carried
In a copper dish her severed breast.
Her steps unslowed
By recent surgery; her body burnished

As an amazon's in goldenrod. The women listen,
Laughing, "Amazons!
We're amazons!"
*
Hail the madrigal that children sing to cheer
Our lady of the bergamot and dew.
And hail protective coloring,
Her famous hooded gaze,
Entering the dreams of followers,
Hunched, parched,
Who cannot hope her breasts will heal them,
But they do. Say it again if it would help.
Would sorrow, holy as her milk, help?
Or prayer in dialect,
Where *breast* still rhymes with *priest?* Try

Whatever smothers the waiting room
And posters of Diahann Carroll, Lee Remick.
Their scarves catch the light.
They give advice. "Check
Your breasts." The nipples, puckered, move,
Saluting stars.
Will they move Lee's photo, since she died?
Although in *Days of Wine and Roses,* in
Anatomy of a Murder, she glows,
Smoothed as cypress wood

Enclosing bodies with delphinium and myrrh.
*
More radiant than you will ever be,
Looking up:
Careful; arms covered, sleeves
Cover where the scars follow hers.

Reflections Lost in the Ladies' Room

Distant flushings sing; run softly; flow,

As ladies wash their hands.
And on to blowers: Wind
On silence through the room and forest-perfumed powder room.
We gather, breathing on beveled glass,

And nurse each other back to life with poise.

And *Rouge Fatàle* and Aqua
Net, "For Lustrous Hold."
"Try mine." "How well you look." She sprays her hennaed
    permanent,
Until the gloss recovers and is stiff.

And she appears improved, concealed with powder.

Flesh is scented with
Carnations. *Touch me not.*
She frowns, with reconstructed dignity. Will she approve
The body, *this is my body,* self-exhumed?

(Even the ones who hurry out without repair
Hear the emphasis:
This is my body,
Do this in memory of me; and at the door,

Glancing back for that familiar body,

They are lost.)
                        *
                   (Remember after the tests,
Mother hid her book
In the cellar, in
The onion smell of wet, collected air; onion tears. And crouched
Down there, I leaned on shelves of jars,

Shy, touching her book. It was banished.

Why Breast Cancer?
Again on the spine.
"One contributor was *stress*." I peeked—a hundred quarrels?
The book smelled old, acid; pages turned,

As if becoming what they were before:

Damp and yellow pulp
From negligible trees.
And where the book opened, glue broke, a shiny ash,
Becoming what it was, I thought,

The horse she was, resting with her trees.

And she was sweat-smeared;
The rubbed trees too.
Her face clouded over when she breathed. For she was opened,
Forced? The cry went hot before it shattered.

"Stress, or *overvigorous intercourse.*"

On her, briefly, on her,

*

                      I saw bruising; breaking
Glass? I was afraid of blood, the same injured body
Asking for camouflage. "For Lustrous Hold."
I showed her where I bled; and broken glass.
She came to me; she ran

Whenever the baby cries.

And I mounted her, mounted what was once a breast
And rode high over the almighty world
And took her away. The remedy of me
With wounds to dress!

For I became her favorite

Wound, intimate as earrings of Philoctetes' bow.)
"How well you look." And flushings sing. "I know."

Temple

Helen Hayes: Another of my pet dreams, despite my inexpressive face, . . . is to be a character actress playing the nurse in Romeo and Juliet, *starring Shirley Temple.*

Mother: My secret ambition is to take a leisurely train trip across the continent and let Shirley greet people at railroad stations.

George Herbert: Was ever grief like mine?

Let her sleep begin with folderol:
A buck-and-wing on TV, by the dancing babe.
Begin with dimpled Temple dolls:
Shirley, teaching Adolphe Menjou how to pray.
She will "not leave you comfortless" "at the codfish ball,"

For she will sing, "Swing Me an Old-Fashioned Song."
Remember "Hey! What Did the Bluejay Say?"
Because your face has not been cheerful, Hall.
Let her sleep.

Hospice nurses let her sleep, turning off
The Temple Festival unearthed on cable.
Turn it back—and marvel at sashays:
Little Princess, Dimples, Little Colonel!
The child who knows her lines knows what to say.
Let her sleep.

*

A funny thing will happen on the way—
That would make her laugh; remember that.
Riddles from the padded hospice chair.

The child who knows her lines knows what to say.
The moment when her temples smell of lanolin
Kiss her hair, haloed in pillows; kiss her there.

*

"I talk to you more than your father."
        And she took me farther toward her,
Hour waking hour, wanting her
        Body back, and I am her. It hurts.

    "A miracle." Her grief was mine.
So button over, mitten up, and learn the lines.
        The child who knows her lines knows what to say.
I laughed, a sound that couldn't wait to fail.

*

Nieces brought embroidered swans from China.
Nurses, Jell-O on an almond-colored tray.

"My daughter will adjust my robe."
Across her feet, "I heard one calling, *Child!*"

And laughed, a sound that couldn't wait to fail.
Can you sing "Animal Crackers"? Can you bite

The heads and hang them up above the bed so high?
And I would kiss her feet, as nurses smooth her robe.

*

"A miracle," said Lionel Barrymore.
            Was ever entertainment
            Such "a splendid thing"?
            Said FDR. "For 15 cents,
            Americans can see
            A baby and forget
            Their troubles"; rotted shoes;
            The family's Chevrolet.

            "The roar of male approval
            Is not for what is sweet,"
            Esquire on *Curly Top*,
            "[But] mocking, hearty—a growl
            Of satisfaction rises
            From the men." A hoopla
            Unashamed as she is,
Singing "Fare-thee-well, Mr. Gloom."

                          *

                  "Depraved,"
Said Graham Greene. "An oddly precocious body,
As voluptuous
            In trousers as Miss Dietrich's.
Infancy is a disguise, and her appeal,
            More secret . . . "

                          *

"Sparkle, Shirley!" Her mother always urged.
   Learn.
Sparkle, dancing baby skin: A tap fiesta.
   Tears.
Sparkle when they want *Our Little Girl.*
   Star.
Sparkle, and the mute in England speak again.
   Again.
"Sparkle, Shirley!" Will you "show me those delights"?
   Why?
Sparkle to the rescue of her sorest need.
   Grieve.
Sparkle, syncopated tapping—
   Faster.
Sparkle when she asks; she asks and eyes brim.
   Blame.
Sparkle and "become as little children."
   Fetch.
Sparkle when I say to sparkle. Sparkle.
   Sparkle.

     *

    I sang
And smiled and wiggled by the bed, so clumsy
   In a salmon robe
   That, this time, she would laugh.

The laughter gathered sheen as it rose,
Too large and unrehearsed. I was afraid
     And laughed,
   A light diversion, as inane
   As teeth around a gasping,
Left with undevoured animals.

     *

Sparkle, Shirley. Other remedies will fail,
From apricots, arsenic, and sharks.
I laughed, a sound that couldn't wait to fail.

*

Lights on the hospice tree will steam in melting snow.
Lights donated in the name of so-and-so.

While we were fearing it, it came—
But came with less of fear
Because that fearing it so long
Had almost made it fair—

—EMILY DICKINSON

Selected for the Mass

Something other than what happened was remembered,
The trees marooned in eyelid-colored air,
Other than the early symptoms missed, and slides
Of what was taken out.
                    At least alive,
Counting cinderblocks around a print of trees.
Humans want impulsive sympathy,
At least *a foliage mirage,* at least a mirage
Of sympathy.
            And want the calm
Expected of survivors, come apart, and scarred,
Quieted, faraway in clean rooms.
A stranger's blood, and lies help—"It won't hurt."
Something for a body—
                    Kiss it; make it better—
Bending to itself, ready for inauguration
To nothing: Little miss fear. Miss flesh.

Descendent

Tell her now   I heard her   *Tell her now*
Mother's voice covered by her hand

I thought I was asleep   drained and slipped in white
The body told me nothing

Nor the doctor's checking sound   Check nod check
Like archaic pelicans pecking their breasts for blood

I thought I was asleep in Mother's voice
Or half-awake   checking

Each sound on me even snow   Did she know it
Did she know how far it spread

Resemblances she knew   Resemblances were beautiful
I heard I had her next recurrence

Her significance   her sores
A body wilder in the cold becoming woe

Her most becoming woe
Will it be removed   frozen or sterilized

Snow skins and swallows up the numb horizon
Sleep   I heard he covered me   *Don't ask for more*

Stamina

The bed, the laminated stand,
With soap on it and towels, folded, four, five,
Piled like snow.

                Snow on hospitals of poured concrete.
                        "It doesn't last." The needle in.
She came. She put the needle in.
The air went out— How fast?

And poison, hung in sacks, began to drip. Poison
Doesn't last.
                Repeated like the objects: Little soaps

                    And towels, damp, and cup.
The nurse will watch it pass and whisper,
"One down." She threw it out
And patted me. Another hung. Her humming. Rounds.

And nothing left
                To vomit. That and that. A stamina
                    In animals; their bodies left.

Snow, flung like puffs of gauze,
Leaned forward, buckled over,
Counting to distract a mattress animal.
Remain erased.

Half-asleep, a snow will bring desire:
Eleven sacks of crocuses
And human smells excused and matted
Down. A snow will break. Six,
Seven after. Fields of celadon will fracture:
Fluid, sky.
The absences, no obstacle to calm.

Was It

Because of too much sun,
The years stretched in sun, yawning,
          What would the doctor say, now,
To those drinking lemonade in Adirondack chairs?

His magazines are old,
The coupons gone for herbal wraps,
          Impurities "extracted through pores."

The dear receptionist: "I told you, she'll be with you in a minute."
Her hands smelled like lilacs,
          Or was it violets? Was it
Wrong to thank her for pleasantries,

The time she gave me from her own new watch?
How soon will the nurse arrive
          And comment optimistically

On mutilated rain or
The body? In a minute, she led me to a smaller room,
          With magazines, with medical
Tips in September's *Woman's Day:*

"30% of patients want to think
It was genetic; the rest, luck . . . " or what they drank, lounging
          In the sun. Was it

Because of too much sun, a baby
On the grass, where freckles burn
        And where the changed ones bleed? Then quick as
    surgery,
A clip, a tuck. And take

The skin and use it over there.
"There you are," and he smiled.
        I heard his other cases, women helped; irrelevant

When they learned to blow air
In their lace prosthetic bras.
        "He smiles, yes," the nurse agreed,
The new one who talks afterwards. How much I could have asked,

And natural to ask,
And to forget their answers; numbers.
        Statistics put the facts to music:

A prognostic lullaby of odds, numbers lulling,
Lulling, nodding off,
        A thousand darkened yawns will flower.
How regressive these desires.

Ink and Green Wash:
In the Oncologist's Waiting Room

Leather banquettes in
Old green edge the room, a drab green of
    Animals, guarded

Under agave on days too hot
To move. Leather banquettes look darker

By the window, by
Rows of warm chrysanthemums.
    The breathing bodies

Wait under reproductions of bamboo.
And leaves point beyond omitted earth

Like autumn feathers,
Laws for flight, falling from the sky.
    Doctors should be told

About the green in waiting rooms.
The walls, green, and green banquettes, as though

Deductive soothing
Could occur. Where are the more explicit
    Chairs, carved with lions,

Scowling and decapitated?
The doctors offer laughter constantly:

Lucy & Ricky
"Leave It to Beaver," and eyes stare,
        Staring back, from fear

Brought forth, only to be unacknowledged.
Lucy & Ricky & Lassie & Timmy

Patty & Cathy
Amos Andy Andy Barney Opie Bee . . .
        A man reads St. Luke,

Slumped on leather; there even darker,
A mark over lips before the kiss arrives.

And days pass, one green
Solid after another, the surface almost split.
        A man reads St. Luke.

Another brings his father back from
Hematology. "Wait here,"

By the wall; he does.
He leans on the door, as bodies give up
        Body languages

To sleep. And when the son returns,
They walk among eyes, walk among eyes,

The easy loathing
Of the body and unspoken wait
        For me, wait for me.

Enter Invisible

If possible, if nurses
Give directions
To modest wig salons; and if

They do go on, the hairs
On enamel, and
On the flannel, cedar-scented pillows,

There are wool hats
And ones of silk
And feathers. Embarrassed for the hair? Hair

That could mend the secret
Nests for children,
Wigs for mockingbirds. Wigs of human

Hair are more expensive.
Add lipstick; lashes,
Lengthened, darkened; rouge; then pencil brows.

A woman without hair
Learns to soothe,
For now, now, with any superstition:

A woman without hair
Is distinguished
By a winding scarf, rising to a crown.

Interior with Metal Instruments

Music—after the walls were washed with irritants
        And after he appears,
Well behind an entourage, all scrubbed in green,
Theatrical authority—

Music swabs and concentrates their talk. The summer
        Meals they most remember:
Carciofi and *carpaccio.* The *Gattinara*
He would recommend, and garlic,

Hawked behind the Duomo and the farther stalls,
        The scarlet eggs in straw
And fair bouquets of marzipan and pitted cherries.
Classic recipes compared:

Whose *insalata di mare* was *the* debauchery?
        On holidays, they are
Aristocrats. And gloved hands will bring them pleasures:
Langoustine and *calamari.*

Mussels crack, fogged in flavored steam that wafts
        Up to spasms; rank
And salty muck, inhaled, burns. "Knife," *Coltello,*
He would tell the boy, expecting

Courtesy. "Yes, sir." The rest tossed in virgin
        Oil from Verona,
Or Firenze's thick chartreuse; or from the coast
Where men could fish, near Porto Fino.

The one the tourists saw returned his nets to foam.
   He nodded toward the room.
Tweezers yank. Metal instruments will pass.
The room has music, enigmatic

As a hand judging stubble poorly shaved.
   The flesh below him, splayed,
Is finally open. Plush inside. He enters sore
Tumescence in the shifting folds,

Twisted wet to gleaming, and he enters under
   Nerves and earliest
Articulations of the pelvis; cuts across
The ligaments and organs gnawed

And hardened; hard to slit. A body takes itself
   By *carcinomatosis;*
Unexpected exponential decadence.
So what? Who watches health,

When this could be a season of abandon, or
   Assault or mockery?
I am taken by his suave and obvious
Superiority; over

And over, carcinomas muscle to the music:
   So mellifluous
A melanoma that we dance. I in backless
Gown, of course, a Mariannette,

And he, *Dottore,* fine in green. We swagger, flesh-
   Voracious, agitated,
Back-lit on the viscous floor. The time together
Wounds. We always soil each other.

Rimbaud's Cancer

The candy striper on her rounds
    Offers paperbacks, then drinks held out
    Like boxing gloves—warm, brown; too flat to hit
The air, or her,
The books she "likes," leaves. The plucky heroine
    Who broke her heel in Abyssinia
Complains.

    I'd turn my face to the wall but everyone does.
       "She turned her face to the wall,"
       The Wings of the Dove.
    Marcel: "At day break, my face still turned to the wall . . . "
So turns the dying woman

    There in a bed across from mine.
More coughing; she calls the nurse.
    Her visitor holds jars of white camellias,
       Odorless as kisses aired on air.
    They shiver when she coughs
And turns; hideous, immense clots—
Disparage to control.

    Garbo coughed more subtly in 1936.
"Jesus!"
    "Nothing by mouth for hours." The nurse leaves.
    "Jesus." Make her stop; deny her pain.
    Then mine begins to dazzle, doesn't it, Rimbaud?

Alone with Isabelle, as she insisted
You were well;
                    Well, or whether you were
Or not, she was not afraid to die. You complained,
        Didn't you, of her enameled crucifix,
                    Or contradicted her?
                    The wrinkles in her coverlet

        Do not approximate a leg.
Her views—
                    Fodder for patter—
On squirrels in holly and the frozen grass
            Were not evidence of paradise.

                    The flocks that bloomed in trees blow off.
                    What happens
            But when it happens to me—
"Jesus, make it stop! Jesus help!"
                    More coughing,
And the visitor will write, "Be good to her."
            "Camellias, Isabelle"—

                    Complain! Stamp "a tiny foot against God."
                    Or bigger, better; suffer
            A big foot to come unto me.
Across linoleum, the nurse's shoes gleam,
                    Approaching stress and stress that perishes.

Bergman's Cancer

I made an effort to amuse, unrattled
By the blind-date manners of the surgeon.
His dewlap shook, with medical abstractions,

A tumor or ectopic pregnancy
He covered when he cleared his throat.
His advice included, "Ontogeny,

Ontology, oncology." "Olé!"
I should have said, topping philosophy
With schoolgirl Spanish; but instead, I poked

My gown, the shade of crumpled silverfish,
Fingered cotton I would call his effigy.
When he would go, when he would say, "Until

Tomorrow—," I would sink, compensatory
Intellect, anatomy-divorced,
Into the international edition of *My Story:*

Ingrid Bergman. A stoic would ignore
Malignancies and emulate *la* perky
Joan of Arc; a cropped, outdoorsy conqueror.

And on her maquillage, *Triage Parfum* . . .
And then immune? Who "amounts to a hill of beans
In this crazy world"? Who in the world

Escapes the accusations of authorities?
Relatives rehearse before they ask—
Before the Ingrid trivia relieves

The afternoon: Ingrid's Anastasia,
And comeback; Ingrid's Oscar; Ingrid's passion;
The Casablanca fog on Ingrid's hat

Crossed the dummy terminal with ash.
When he returns, "I'm no good at being noble,"
With his endearments of suspicious origin and

Charm that will improve the more that he controls,
I let him "think for me," hill and all,
Loving dampered nonsense on piano.

St. Peregrinus' Cancer

His miracles abbreviated, *Lives of Saints*
    Elaborates his pain:
The famous field he crossed, obliquely, like a crab.
    Silver-pointed crickets
Fanned away, hiding from his dogwood stick,
    His cap on auburn grass.
The clover smelled of local wine, and there
    His vanity could end.

The caption, "Byzantine and Mediterranean,"
    Appeared in my edition
As "Bizarre and sweaty." He was bizarre and sweaty
    Crossing the field in pain.
The parables he hoped the baffled children would
    Recite turned back to babble.

And grass *was not unlike* his doubt, scorched and growing.
    Not silent or silenced,
Nor what in such despair would silence silence—translated
    "He liked to be alone."
An audience today would understand. He went
    The other way; his name
Meant "crossing the field"; going away, one-legged
    In wild licorice.

He sneezed, ruining his pretty suffering,
      The patron saint of cancer.
Once I asked for his crisis, tattooed on my thigh.
      A conversation piece,
Approachable: "Hello. I see by your thigh
      You want to be alone."

Or "Haven't we met? I know your thigh is not unlike
      My own . . . " A mock-romantic
Brutalism elected with these mutilations.
      And then declare "Cut here,"
To pierce: A gouge for cloisonné; a drowsy blue
      Carves in skin, *"my love."*
My mother chronicled her cobalt, chemo,
      Then tamoxifen.

Her years of this; her " '*Bravery,*' the doctors said."
      We picked at crab imperials.
I wished for more. I couldn't help it, imagining
      A swoon in cold moiré.
Have and overcome, have and overcome,
      And then I did. I had

The diagnosis; surgery; a souvenir of stitches,
      Pink-stemmed flushes,
Shades of plasma; doubled burgundies and dusky
      Roses; weltered flesh;
The mottled violet and flattened mauve corsages;
      Burnt sienna tissue;
Hardy musk and moss maroon; Madame de Pompadour,
      Ancestor rose! We laughed,

A ladies' lunch, where overarcing hats with velvet
       Clover met; a field
I'd never seen before. The undulating veils
       Of air and grass became
"You're thin, so thin, so thin, so thin, so thin," so then,
       We were alike, at last.

I was on my way to mother. And from time to time I said, Mother, to encourage me I suppose. I kept losing my hat, the lace had broken long ago, until in a fit of temper I banged it down on my skull with such violence that I couldn't get it off again. And if I had met any lady friends, if I had had any lady friends, I would have been powerless to salute them correctly.

—SAMUEL BECKETT

Mother

If I THOUGHT I needed her—but some things happen
Without thinking or written permission. You hate to admit it.
I do too! I drank "too much" of her, she whispered,
Listing my "*infractions,*"
And if I made her nipples bleed, then here began
The taste for blood I later took as my one advantage.
She said, "I knew I wouldn't die; you needed me,"
As if my dependence
Were adrenaline, pumping her up another year,
Overactive *for me;* and so she wouldn't die?
Her glands laughed at this hypothesis, squirting
Estrogen at my
Ignorance. I kicked myself for needing a *mother,*
Kicked a chunk of skin off, KICKED with cleated shoes,
A kick-off acrobatic punishment. And bruises
In the weeks to come
Added a color to my life I had avoided.
Even in adversity I planned ahead.
And missed her (a premature nostalgia); she wasn't dead.
I missed her avalanche
Of language, SOUND opinions she poured on me, inflected
Wishes to persuade, or satiate, instead
Of listening in conversation; days done,
Smothered; mother WON.
Then I shared her victory; I sipped approval, aped
Approval (b*itch*) & clitoral [self-]confidence.
[Her] desires, eyed, feared, galled; [never] forgiven.
[Her] incessant JABS
& kisses, a legacy (a m*enace*). More naps,
Neglected [for] overbearing parturition. . . . [She] quelled

45

Riots [she] provoked (retaliation, *rapport*).
Remember her scent,
Then? The usual vituperation, waspish xxxs,
Yielding [she seemed to yield, to the wrong, wiley] youth,
[She] gazed . . . a zone I loathed, loved, knew, used
To want to emulate,
Until she sniffed out my impudent growth, my "INDEPENDENCE,"
Incipient resemblance to a faux-adult.
For how *adult* is it to wander lonely as a fool,
Slouching toward snowy woods
So often in the middle of the journey, you could ask,
If it is a destiny, an ambulatory thrust, why stop, why
Are you afraid again in the middle of your life?
The old woods are happy
To receive derivative anxieties.
Inhale each one, with the wet wood smell,
Hyperventilating, yes fainting, overwhelmed.
Sic semper tyrannis:
The only loved mother is a dead mother.
Leaves rustle in proverbial enthusiasm,
La, la, a preverbal dawdle. Leaves loosen under
A skinned sky; most
Lost . . . to hysteria, in the way out of the womb-orama.
I packed my dancing shoes to dance the dance of death,
Shiniest scarlet spikes, humming, *Free at last,*
But it didn't last, alas.
Alas! Excuse *me,* my bowels insist—such pain,
Crippling; doubled over (DOUBLED!), near-collapse
      Within the ladies' room I call home. No pus?
      Blood? Thank God, for anal-
      Analysis, mastered rapidly with mirrors.
      How ridiculous did I appear? As if
      I were objective alone; as if baby chirping
      In winter were meditative.

On the toilet, excrementally inspired,
Aspiring to perspire, sentenced to ask, why
Is THOUGHT grammatical—for God, Mother, Whatever-
Better-Listener
Supposed to linger as afterimage, soul, or
Über-explicator of what I *tried* here
To SAY [with the door shut decisively] and urine
Falling through the world,
Finding a way out, free of the wide body:
If urine be the mood of love—pee on!
Fall far into the gathered water and good-bye.
Farewell, mes amigos!
The wee ones tumble gold from the cold hills above.
They never despair, though diluted, flushed away,
And who knows where, what darkness, sea-dissolved,
What terrible escape?
Enough; 'tis not so sweet now as it was before.
Where was I? I could not arrive fast enough.
Birds showed how easy it was to move over
The overarcing trees, if
You were a bird; but you are not; nor I; so I
Heaved a phlegmy sigh, adding to my list
Affronts & consequent furies: "Movement, Constricted"
And entered the huge light:
La magnificence. I expected nothing less
And tightened bandages on raw epidermis.
Infections ooze, exposed; exposed, who wouldn't diminish?
Wrapped in one long piece
Of surgical gauze, no one could say I am not in ONE piece.
Head wrapped; neck wrapped; nose wiped; breasts reconstructed,
Lifted as a wisp of a girl would have 'em: conic icons,
The latest silicone nipples;
Tummy-tucked and buttocks wrapped, nay, deified,
I am luminous as any gaze I meet.

I meet the morning, and I—every bit as glamorous
As light in my dazzling gauze—
Dismiss ambiguous murmurings as wind.
"I have my own wind to worry about," I hiss,
Boldly, enlarged by tact; absorbed in fartlessness.
No empathy, no ART.
Gauze sags and flaps around my bound ankles,
Giving passersby a chuckle, without THANKS.
I tip my hat—an art in itself—and wish them ill,
Very ill, malignant.
"Horses sweat, men perspire, and women glow,"
Said mother vibrantly, once upon a time.
"Excessive sweating is not what we wish for horses"—I
Gained my own glow
Correcting her. Pedantry is a poor triumph,
Hardly a triumph, a pinched-nerve self-righteousness
From dictionaries pawed, pawed for the bitter, first
Roots of conversation.
Better a solitude of bitter herbs than her?
Better to be bitter than batter a parent's heart?
Better belched than regretted? Better wretched than left?
Better alone? Better?
Perpetual silence with her is the best defense.
The feeble mystery of the socially inept.
Where am I? The road changed and trees bent back
Where I was. I—asked
For interruption; didn't visit her yesterday,
Exhausted by the trauma of her dying. Nights,
I fell to yawning, proving my point. I've been this far
Before, broke off and cried
By a large yellow moon-faced rock. I cried on the rock,
Dripping a slow ticking sound, awkwardly,
And thought any stranger's sympathy would end my grief,
Amputate its reason,

And the scabbed, engorged stump I kept over
The years? I thought it was seductive as a girl's
Tears, as the gauze loosened for decolletage;
And visibly cold.
I thought shivering would tantalize intruders:
A hero hovering, a mother-surrogate,
A man who mothers pampers; papa warms and offers
To the estranged daughter
Six pomegranate seeds, six plucked pills
To swallow. And she gathers, in the first gasp
Recognized, her plump opiated spasms:
Taken on, in,
Exhaled, hailed, pricked with numberless pervasions,
All dissolve resolves roughened, more delicious.
It changed underground. He had her punctuated
Once. He did it once?
And she was thinking of her mother at the time.
I cannot recommend (to lady friends) too highly
A rumination in the road; inhale the earth,
The cold particulars,
And smell the road where it digresses under trees.
I did it without fainting, vomiting; such progress.
Up the hill, women hug; a partial hug
Again before they part.
Why do women enter the world in pairs, when
They enter the world at all? I watch their silhouettes,
(Wrenching my neck muscle friend Rhomboideus)
A didactic voyeurism.
I peeped for truth. One turns the other's cheek
For rouge advice—armor readied for the world.
Must they wear each other's feathered hats for luck?
How far into the world
Will they—Do I regret not doing what they do?
Do - be - do - be - do . . . What do they do?

Do I want them to be as hesitant as I am?
I envy their abandon,
How they wipe their blood on roses, worms, without regret,
And birds take the warm, sweet spots for suet.
To be woman-fattened for winter and not become her
Lowest common denominator
Equal. Nothing. Fatigue accomplished,
Fatigue, the beautiful other cheek of aggression.
I sing under a snarl of winter trees *revenge,*
Instead of doing a thing.
Stasis? Thy name is "long-standing rage arrested":
Rage clotted in the blood and calling home.
Home to MOTHER then, walking up slowly
Past the winter roses,
The pairs of women out of rage. Where will I be?
> Which guards will doctors post at her door this evening?
> They are democratic in attentiveness,
> Though smug. *"Ho, there!"*
> I bang against one, in purely filial haste, bang,
> Now that I think of it, more than etiquette
> Requires. BANG BANG BANG, to be exact;
> Hardly pure; lurid?
> Stumbling (not responsible?), or in a spirit
> Of feminist body CONTROL, I choose to bang him,
> But choose not, I confess, the consequences:
> A brain aroused for battle,
> A body masturbating for autonomy.
> I delay, a heap of odors routed beneath,
> Above? (prepositionally entangled with?) her deathbed scene.
> Never visiting,
> Nor cradling her, when blood was extracted from her lungs,
> I was useless. "Yes, you make NOTHING happen,"
> Mother sighed from her many mattresses.
> *PUFF, PUFF, PUFF,*

She was still a wise, oxygen example.
I kneeled by her bed, not helping her, sad.
Hearing her distant, ever-weaker breathing, near the sky,
And raised to be a child,
I needed her; and petted her robe, unsatisfied,
Slipping it round me, pitying my knees, and rose.
Humans revel in their tender usefulness,
In some concocted purpose.
And if I lay me down to sleep beside her (not there—
Wait—I ran around her bed, for a bigger pillow)
And pray for her to die or me to wake, but prayer
Was answered years ago.

Then light a light cigarette in celebration.
(Dangers to your health are mollified in bed.)
And gaze out the window, as if you owned the view,
The winter afternoon,
The light a warmer color, orange, as it dies.
Her bed warms, when movement is constricted to this end,
To breath in fetal paradise and leisure resurrected,
Tit alternative:
The orange ash brightens to my breath, approaches.
Let the light approach, and I wave away the smoke,
Imperial command; her mannerism: cigarettes
For emphasis, italics,
Ashes: another atheist's illusion of angels:
Ashes everywhere, like angels for emphasis.

        "I think not!" twin nurses cry ("Too ad hominem,"
I thought defensively,
Rattled by consensus, as they outnumber and
Unswaddle, heave me out—) without professional banter.
No "we understand how you feel"; no courtesy-pity.
They hand me a six-page bill—

The final affront. Or punishment? Epiphany?
—And kick me out. They throw something after me,
Lock the door, as my jaw drops, a version of awe.
And light there in the hall
Is gone and light beyond; there, the farther windows
Darken; others; until the moon and thinning snow
And shapes intuited are all there is. The road,
Soundless, moonlight, sewn.

To Come with Accessories

1

Inherited: The opals set in cuffs.
    They match the layered moonlight crêpe de chine.
Or earrings dangle emeralds; or come
    With silver strands, with pendant tourmalines;
With head flung back, the body damp with gold dust
    And the power implied. Arrive in opal cuffs
        And crêpe de chine, with patent leather heels
          Reflecting up, up
The fragrant skin, the lingeried pudendum.
        Each clasp and each unclasping is mine,
And means nothing, but more of her desired.

2

"That always makes me cry." And I would need
    A handkerchief from the beaded evening bag
Inherited, and for a moment, I would need
    This air in the labyrinth
And cul-de-sacs of bearded irises.
    The evening underestimates the tears:
        The customary repertoire of welling up
        And over centuries.
Tears form a white-on-white oasis
    For the time alone. Ridiculous again.
Nauseated and in need of wiping, and still alone.

3

And panic could be made to seem absurd:
    A girlish vestige, silly tears. They ring
The garden cushions with traditional despair.
    And mourners come in sodden coteries
With their embraces, with tears they will compare
    And frame in ormolu. And for how long
        Are they immersed in the Symphony in Big C,
        Die Grosse Melancholie,
And protected by elaboration from farewell?
    She died. And the appalling quiet; absence.
Sorrow longs for abstraction, not farewell.

4

Far far from the body
    Who led me to lie down
And she is gone
    Holy by default
And far from the fear shouted
    A cacophony appended to the sky
        To signify or else
            Inoculate from silence
Far far from the body
    Holy by default
I am a body in ash-blonde smoke, aroused alone.

A Little April

Water broke on the woven backs of summer chairs.
A boy who never knew her ran in the changing air
And vanishes in foliage and iron foliage.
The path is scented with serrated hedges
And grass mounded by the gate. It doesn't matter.
Whatever reaches out could be rejected.
He was kind that one minute. I remember one,
Instinctively accounting to protect myself,
As if protection were some last word in love.
Water broke on the woven backs of summer chairs.

Notes

The Monarch Birthmark: "Should insects get dry and stiff before they are spread, they must be relaxed. This is done by putting them in a covered jar." Frank E. Lutz, *Field Book of Insects* (Putnam, 1948).

Touched Relics: "Snobbery however was not the only reason for the virtual disappearance of the nursing Madonna. Purity's alliance with modesty, and shame at the naked female body's beauty, contributed. It became indecorous for the Virgin to bare her breasts. . . . Tears are the only bodily effluvium permitted in an age obsessed with physical well-being and with the influence of the body on the personality. Snot, spit, blood, milk, nail parings, hairs all inspire recoil." Marina Warner, *Alone of All Her Sex: The Myth and the Cult of the Virgin Mary* (Knopf, 1976).

Temple: "Again and again Mother's instructions included the word 'sparkle.' Arching eyebrows and rounding the mouth in an expression of surprise was 'sparkling,' by her definition. So was frowning with an outthrust lower lip. . . . It was a word covering a total attitude, an emotional stance. When she said 'sparkle' it meant energy, an intellectual intensity." Shirley Temple Black, *Child Star: An Autobiography* (Warner Books, 1988).

"Her mother taught her to 'sparkle' as she called it, by wetting her lips, focusing her eyes so that they gleamed with a little pre-tearing moisture." Anne Edwards, *Shirley Temple: American Princess* (William Morrow, 1988).

"A young girl from Romford, England, named Kathleen Robinson, congenitally mute for twelve years, became so excited watching the film [*Bright Eyes*] that her ability to speak was suddenly restored." Shirley Temple Black, *Child Star: An Autobiography*.

"I lost an old friend. That's how I refer to my mastectomy. But that was 22 years ago. Just after surgery [1972], I held a news conference and got the word out, telling women not to be afraid. I was the first celebrity to go public with her breast cancer. I felt that I could help my sisters." Shirley Temple Black, *Life* (May, 1994).

"The use of laetrile or amygdalin for the treatment of cancer is under investigation.... Amygdalin ... occurs in seeds of *Rosaceae*, especially in almonds and apricots seeds." Ewen Cameron and Linus Pauling, *Cancer and Vitamin C* (The Linus Pauling Institute of Science and Medicine, 1979). See also *Sharks Don't Get Cancer*, by Dr. William Lane and Linda Comac (Publishers Group West, 1992).

Lines 33 and 68 are from George Herbert's "The Collar" and "Heaven," respectively.

Ink and Green Wash: In the Oncologist's Waiting Room: "NASA aggressively studies how plants reduce pollutants because astronauts must deal with toxic emissions from synthetic material on spaceships. Based on their research, the best plant for the job can be found in the chart below ... FORMALDEHYDE in household cleaners: chrysanthemum; BENZENE in plastics: chrysanthemum; TRICHLORO-ETHYLENE in inks: chrysanthemum." "For Our Customers," *Bank of America* (January, 1993).

Interior with Metal Instruments: *"The robustness of French common names:* ... Marianne Lavergne, Mariette Borelly, Mariannette Laugier ... *Household Sadism:* at Marseilles, Sade wants Marianne Lavergne to whip him with a parchment beater with bent pins which he takes from his pocket. The girl quails before so exclusively functional an object (like a surgical instrument), and Sade orders the maidservant to bring a *heather broom;* this utensil is more familiar to Marianne and she has no hesitation in employing it to strike Sade across the buttocks." Roland Barthes, *Sade/Fourier/Loyola,* translated by Richard Miller (Farrar, Straus and Giroux, 1976).

Rimbaud's Cancer: "The tubercular could be an outlaw or a misfit; the cancer personality is regarded more simply, and with condescension, as one of life's losers. Napoleon, Ulysses S. Grant, Robert A. Taft, and Hubert Humphrey have all had their cancer diagnosed as the reaction to political defeat and the curtailing of their ambitions. And the cancer deaths of those harder to describe as losers, like Freud and Wittgenstein, have been diagnosed as the gruesome penalty exacted for a lifetime of instinctual renunciation. (Few remember that Rimbaud died of cancer.)" Susan Sontag, *Illness As Metaphor* (Random House, 1979).

Bergman's Cancer: "She [Ingrid Bergman] was so shy about saying what it was at the time; ten years ago dying of breast cancer and being ashamed, not saying it was breast cancer, because the idea of the breast was sexual, or too intimate, or too dirty, not elegant." Isabella Rossellini, interview in *Vogue* (January, 1993).

St. Peregrinus' Cancer: St. Peregrinus Laziosi (also St. Peregrine Laziosi), 1260–1345. "A great affliction now befell him in the form of cancer of the foot, which, besides being excruciatingly painful, made him an object of repulsion to his neighbours. He bore this trial without a murmur. At last the surgeons decided that the only thing to do was to cut off the foot. St. Peregrine spent the night before the operation in trustful prayer; he then sank into a light slumber, from which he awoke completely cured—to the amazement of the doctors, who testified that they could no longer detect any trace of the disease. . . . It is said that for thirty years he never sat down." Butler's *Lives of the Saints,* vol. 2 (Christian Classics, Inc., 1981).

Mother: Line 81 is from William Shakespeare's *Twelfth Night; Or, What You Will,* act 1, scene 2, lines 7–8.

To Come with Accessories: "Isn't there a good image in John Wayne beating cancer? Sure, I licked the Big C." John Wayne, press conference (1964).

The Ohio State University Press/ *The Journal* Award in Poetry
DAVID CITINO, Poetry Editor

1996	John Haag	Stones Don't Float: Poems Selected and New
1995	Fatima Lim-Wilson	Crossing the Snow Bridge
1994	David Young	Night Thoughts and Henry Vaughan
1993	Bruce Beasley	The Creation
1992	Dionisio D. Martínez	History as a Second Language
1991	Teresa Cader'	Guests
1990	Mary Cross	Rooms, Which Were People
1989	Albert Goldbarth	Popular Culture
1988	Sue Owen	The Book of Winter
1987	Robert Cording	Life-list

The George Elliston Poetry Prize

1987	Walter McDonald	The Flying Dutchman
1986	David Weiss	The Fourth Part of the World
1985	David Bergman	Cracking the Code